RHINOS

Written and edited by **Lucy Baker**

Consultant Douglas Richardson
London Zoo

TWO-CAN

First published in Great Britain in 1991 by
Two-Can Publishing Ltd
27 Cowper Street
London EC2A 4AP

Typesetting by The Creative Text Partnership
Printed in Italy by Amadeus – Rome

British Library Cataloguing in Publication Data
Baker, Lucy
Rhinos.
I. Rhinos
I. Title
599.728

ISBN 1-85434-044-1

Photographic Credits:
Front Cover Tony Stone Photolibrary – London p.4 Gerald Thompson/Oxford Scientific Films p.5 Bob Campbell/Survival Anglia p.6 (left) Leonard Lee Rue/Bruce Coleman Ltd. (right) Ian Beames/Ardea p.7 (top) McDougal/Ardea (bottom) Kenneth W. Fink/Ardea p.8-9 Peter Johnson/NHPA p.10-11 Nigel Dennis/NHPA p.12 Alan Weaving/ Ardea p.13 Dieter & Mary Plage/Bruce Coleman Ltd. p.14 Satan Osolinski/Oxford Scientific Films p.15 (top) Leonard Lee Rue/Bruce Coleman Ltd. (bottom) Stephen Krasemann/NHPA p.16 Michael Price/Bruce Coleman Ltd. p.17 (top) Stephen Krasemann/NHPA (bottom) Dr. Charles McDougal/Ardea p.18 Anthony Bannister/NHPA p.19 Jen & Des Bartlett/Survival Anglia.

Illustration Credits:
Back Cover p.4-19 David Cook/Linden Artists p.20-21 Steve Ling/Linden Artists p.22-23 Claire Legemah p.24-25 Ken Hooks/Jeremy Clegg p.26-30 Clive Pritchard/ Linden Artists p.31 Alan Rogers.

CONTENTS

LOOKING AT RHINOS

Rhinos are huge, thick-skinned animals. They have solid, barrel-shaped bodies and short, stocky legs. Most people compare the rhino to the hippo, but its closest relative is the horse. The rhino's full name is rhinoceros.

Each rhino is heavily armed. It has one or two slightly curving horns that grow from the top of its nose. Rhino horns are not made of ivory like elephant tusks. They are made of keratin, which is also found in claws, hair and fingernails.

Although rhinos have roamed free for millions of years, their future is uncertain. They are among the most endangered of all large mammals. Only small populations of rhinos survive in parts of Africa and Asia.

▲ Rhinos have round, tapering tails that end in small tufts of hair. Their eyes are small but their ears are large and they have very long noses.

► The rhino's horns look like fearsome weapons but, in truth, rhinos are more likely to run from trouble than stand and fight. Rhinos' horns grow like fingernails throughout the animals' lives.

RHINO FACTS

The largest rhinos can weigh over 3,000 kg (3 tons). Out of all the animals on land, only elephants are heavier.

The rhino's large, funnel shaped ears can be swivelled to catch sound from a chosen direction.

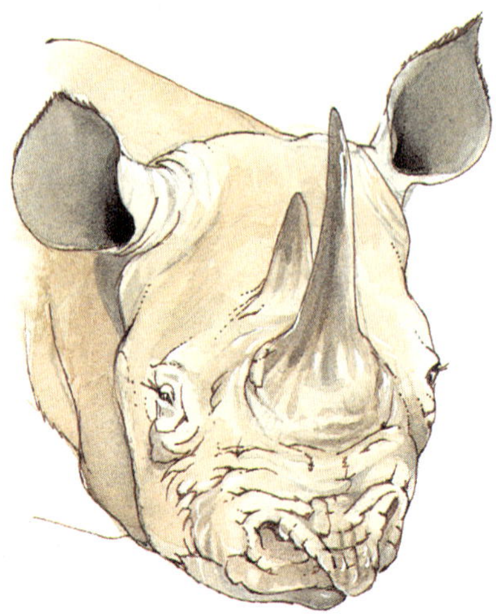

The largest rhino horn on record was over two metres (six feet) long.

AFRICAN OR ASIAN?

There was once a vast and varied number of rhinos. Today, only five different species exist throughout the world. Two of the surviving species of rhino live in Africa, and the other three live in parts of Asia.

Africa's two rhino groups are called black rhinos and white rhinos. The names are not very useful as both groups are a similar grey colour. The easiest way to tell black rhinos and white rhinos apart is to compare the shape of their lips.

Both African rhinos have longer horns than their Asian cousins. The white rhinos' horns are the longest. They are also the largest animals of the surviving five species.

Asia's rhinos include the Great Indian one-horned rhino, the Javan rhino and the Sumatran rhino. The Great Indian one-horned rhino is famed for its heavily folded skin which is partly covered in small, round lumps. Both the Javan and the Sumatran rhinos are very rare.

◀ The best way to tell the two African rhinos apart is to look at the animal's lips. The white rhino has flat lips and is sometimes called the square-lipped rhino.

▼ The black rhino has a more pointed jaw line. It is sometimes called the long-lipped rhino.

▲The Great Indian one-horned rhino is easily recognised. Its skin hangs in definite folds around the body and is marked in places by small, round lumps. Early explorers thought that the Indian rhino was wearing a suit of armour, and that the round lumps of skin were rivets, which showed where the suit was held together.

▶ The Sumatran rhino is the smallest and most primitive of all rhino groups. Unlike other rhinos, it has a thin hairy coat. The young Sumatran rhino in this picture is just beginning to grow its horns.

THE RHINO'S HOME

Rhinos live in tall, swampy grasslands, forested slopes and open bush lands. They are usually shy, peaceful animals.

Each rhino lives within an area called its home range. Females may share parts of their ranges, but most males keep clear boundaries between their homes.

Rhinos mark out their territory by spraying urine on paths and borders, scraping over sites with their legs and horns, and using regular dung heaps. Some rhinos have communal dung heaps that are used by all the rhinos in the neighbourhood.

The size of a rhino's home range depends on the amount of food and water available in its area. In the open Namib Desert individual rhinos occupy vast tracts of land, whereas in India many rhinos will share a small area of dense elephant grass.

Occasional fights break out between rhinos, especially males.

Most battles involve a number of ritualised movements and neither animal gets hurt, but sometimes fighting can be fierce.

African rhinos jab upwards with their horns when they are fighting. Asian rhinos use their sharp front teeth to attack an opponent.

Black rhinos have a reputation as the most aggressive rhinos. They are well known for their unprovoked charges.

▼ Two male white rhinos wrestle with their horns. This ritualised fighting proves the senior position of the male that holds its own territory.

RHINO RITUALS

African rhinos regularly sharpen their horns by rubbing them on trees or rocks.

Charging rhinos can reach a speed of up to 50 km an hour (30 miles an hour).

Rhinos' communal dung heaps are called middens. In Africa, rhino middens can be over five metres (16 feet) wide.

WALLOWING

Rhinos cannot sweat to keep cool. Instead, they lie in wet mud. This is called wallowing, and it is the rhino's favourite pastime.

Rhinos like to stay submerged for many hours at a time. When they finally leave their wallows, they have wet mud coats that cool their bodies down as the mud dries. The rhino's mud coat also provides a protective layer between the animal's skin and biting insects.

In Africa, there is not always enough water to wallow in. During dry spells, African rhinos roll on sandy or gritty ground to keep themselves clean.

Water is much more readily available to Asian rhinos because they live in wetter climates. The great Indian one-horned rhinos have large, public wallows where several animals may gather at noon and stay until sunset.

MEAL TIMES

Rhinos eat most of their food at the beginning and end of the long tropical day. They have to eat a huge amount to meet their daily requirements.

Rhinos do not eat other animals. Instead they eat leaves, twigs and grasses. Sometimes they feed on fallen fruit and underground roots.

The diet of the two African rhinos depends on the shape of their mouths. The white rhinos graze like cows on new grass shoots with their square lips. The black rhinos pick leaves and twigs with their pointed lips.

The Indian rhino can use its lips to pick at slender twigs and long grasses or fold its lips away to graze on short grass shoots.

Both Javan and Sumatran rhinos live in thick forest where they feed on twigs and fallen fruit. Like the black rhinos, they will 'walk down' small trees and bushes to reach the upper leaves.

DRINKING FACTS

Asian rhinos need to drink every day but African rhinos can survive for a few days at a time without water. During periods of drought, African rhinos may have to dig the ground to find water. They use their front feet for digging but may unearth roots and bulbs with their horns.

◀ The white rhinos use their square lips to graze like cows on new grass shoots. In cool weather white rhinos feed and rest throughout the day but if it is hot they eat most of their food during the night.

▶ The rare Javan rhino lives in thick forest where it feeds on a variety of twigs, leaves and fallen fruit. Once hunted for damaging farmers' crops, the Javan rhino is now protected by law.

BABY RHINOS

Female rhinos begin mating when they are about five or six years old. Thereafter, they give birth to a single rhino every two to four years.

Baby rhinos are called calves. They look like miniature versions of their parents without the horns. Young rhinos begin growing horns when they are a few months old.

Rhino calves can stand and walk within ten minutes of birth. They communicate with their mothers in whines and squeals.

Rhino mothers stay with their offspring for nearly two years after the birth. They are fiercely protective of the growing calves. It is not until female rhinos have mated and are due to give birth again that they dismiss their young. Young rhinos may join a childless female before they choose to live alone.

▲ A mother and calf play with each other by rubbing horns. They communicate by making various sounds or leaving scent messages. Growing rhinos live with their mothers for at least the first two years of their lives.

CALF FACTS

Most rhino calves weigh about 40 kg (90 pounds) at birth, more than ten times the weight of a human baby.

White rhinos stand over their offspring if danger threatens.

Rhinos live up to 40 years in captivity but probably have shorter lives in the wild.

▲ A mother rhino and her calf are never parted during their first months together, but the way the two animals travel differs. Black rhino calves follow a few paces behind their mothers, whereas Indian and white rhino calves nearly always travel a short distance in front of their mothers.

▶ A young calf suckles milk from its mother. Female rhinos can produce over 20 litres (35 pints) of milk a day while they are raising their young. Rhino calves continue to drink their mother's milk for about a year, but grasses or leaves are added to their diet when the calves are a few weeks old.

NEIGHBOURS

Rhinos share their homes with a wide variety of animals but they have few natural enemies. Normally, they live peacefully with their neighbours and are neither predators nor prey.

The creatures that give rhinos the most trouble are tiny biting insects. Over 20 different varieties of ticks alone have been found feeding on a black rhino's back.

Birds such as the oxpecker and cattle egret pick insects from the rhino's body. Although they help keep down the number of pests, the birds' constant pecking can upset rhinos.

Large predators, like lions and packs of hyenas in Africa and tigers in Asia, pose little threat to adult rhinos. They may prey on calves that are left unguarded by their mothers or attack a very sick rhino, but they avoid healthy adults.

There have been reports of both crocodiles and hippos attacking rhinos but this is very rare.

▼ Birds like the cattle egret and oxpecker visit rhinos to feed on the biting insects that live on their skin. Turtles have also been seen picking pests off rhinos' bodies when they are wallowing in lakes or rivers.

▲ The lion, so-called King of Beasts, will not challenge an adult rhino. The lion in this picture is on the retreat from a charging black rhino. The rhino is unlikely to attack. It will simply frighten the lion away.

▶According to African folklore, elephants and rhinos are sworn enemies and there are several accounts of African elephants killing rhinos. In India, however, the elephants are scared of rhinos and run away from them if approached. Some Indian national parks have trained elephants to stand their ground so that people can study rhinos from the animals' backs.

RHINO PROBLEMS

Today, rhinos are one of the most endangered animal groups. Out of the five remaining species, four are on the verge of extinction. There are many reasons for the rhino's decline.

In parts of Africa, whole rhino populations have disappeared during periods of drought. Elsewhere the animals have lost their homelands to farmers and developers. More particularly, rhinos have been shot by hunters and poachers.

A small number of rhinos have always been hunted for meat and raw materials. However, since the invention of the gun, they have been killed in huge numbers. In the early 1900s, rhinos were shot for sport by hunters. Now they are killed for their valuable horns by poachers.

International laws have been made to protect rhinos and restrict trade in their horns. Nevertheless, some people continue to poach rhinos, and rhino numbers are dwindling.

The Javan rhino population is the smallest. At the last count, it was estimated that there were no more than 50 of these rare mammals. White rhinos are the most numerous. There are more than 3,000 white rhinos in Africa's national parks.

▲ Some rhinos are taken from their wild homes and introduced to national parks. Inside the parks, rhinos can be protected from poachers and studied by scientists.

◀ Drastic measures have been taken to stop poachers killing rhinos. In parts of Africa there is outright war between game wardens and poachers. Here, a black rhino has been put to sleep so that its horns can be removed. It is hoped that the hornless rhino will be spared from the poachers' guns.

RHINO PRODUCTS

In China and other eastern countries, people believe the rhino has magical qualities. Rhino products, such as horns, skin, blood and urine, are sold for high prices to be used in various medicines.

Rhino horns are used to make the handles of ceremonial daggers called jambias. These are given to the sons of wealthy Muslims in Yemen. Although the handles of jambias can be made from other materials, huge sums of money are paid for genuine rhino-horn handles. This encourages people to spend time and money hunting rhinos in Africa.

BUSH GAME

START
Run from warden's truck. On 3 spaces.
Stop to browse in the thicket. Miss a go.
Take short cut to avoid hyenas.
Stop to roll on ground. Miss a go.
Chased on by male rhino. Move on 2 spaces.
Pick up mother's scent. Hurry on 3 spaces.

Can you help the young black rhino find his mother? You will need a dice and some counters to play this game.

BE CAREFUL – if you land on a black square you have to start again.

RHINO MASK

Try making a mask. You will need a piece of cardboard or thick paper, a length of elastic or string and a pair of scissors.

Draw and carefully cut out the basic mask shape. Remember to make two holes for your eyes and a small hole at each side of the mask. Decorate your mask and then thread a piece of elastic or string through the holes at the sides. Now your mask is ready to wear!

There are lots of ways to decorate masks. Here are a few things to try.

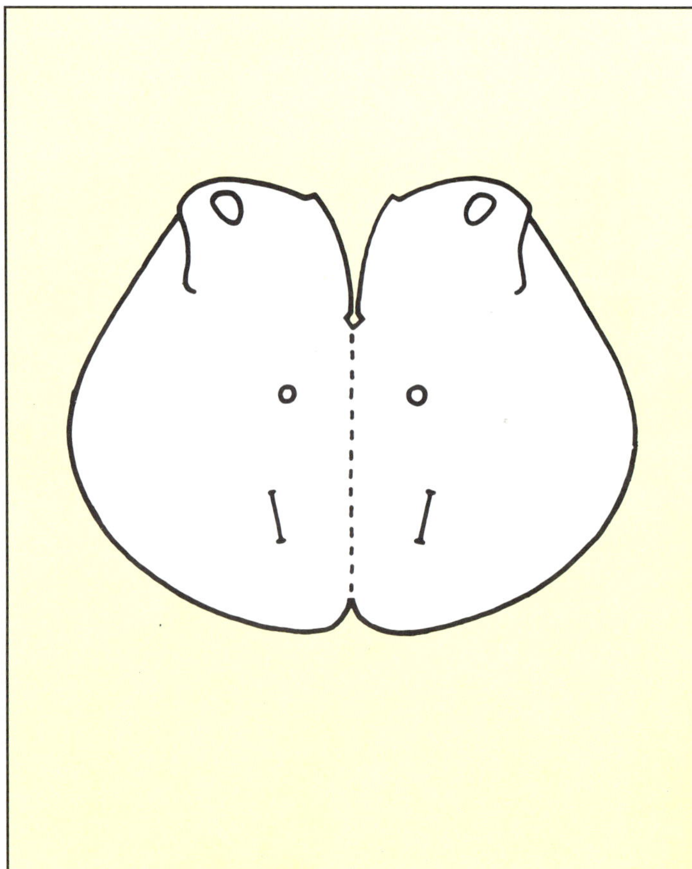

▶ Our mask was made by cutting out this basic shape from cardboard and adding paper shapes.

FIND THE RHINOS

There are six rhinos hiding in this picture. Can you find them?

There is one more animal in the picture. Do you know its name?

THE RHINO LOSES ITS HORNS

BY CLIVE FARNDON

Ralph is a black rhino. He lives with his mother, Rosie, in Damaraland. Damaraland is a dry fringe of land between the desert and the Skeleton Coast of Namibia in Africa. This is an unusual place to find black rhinos because it is difficult for them to survive on the edge of a desert.

Ralph is nearly one year old. His mother is teaching him all the skills she knows for survival – what he can eat, where to find water and how to avoid danger in his desert home.

Rosie and Ralph have just been rolling in the mud at a local waterhole. Mud helps to keep rhinos cool and is good for their skins. Usually Rosie and Ralph have to make do with a dustbath.

Now mother and son are in search of some tasty welwitschia plants. The leaves of these gigantic plants are their favourite food, although Ralph still likes to drink his mother's milk when she lets him.

Ralph trots behind his mother and she begins to tell him about people.

Ralph learns that people are easy to recognise. They are not the same as other animals. They travel the desert in noisy, fast vehicles. On the rare occasions that they leave their vehicles, people walk on their back legs.

Rosie tells Ralph there are two types of people: the good ones and the bad ones. The bad people are called poachers. They kill animals with stick-like objects called guns and then steal their horns or skins.

Ralph does not like the sound of poachers. To reassure him, Rosie tells him about the good people, the game wardens. They too have guns but they do not use them on the animals. Instead, the game wardens use their guns to scare off poachers.

Suddenly a loud and noisy bird, bigger than Ralph has ever seen, comes swooping down towards them. His mother tosses her great head with a snort and thunders off. Ralph tosses his little head, tries to snort and runs after her as quickly as he can.

The bird, which is actually a helicopter, swoops after them. It passes so low and so loud that Ralph is sure there can be no escape. Then it steers away and comes down to land with a bump.

By now Ralph has almost caught up with his mother. She has slowed to a clumsy trot. He thinks she seems a little unsteady. Then he notices a brightly coloured feather dart in her rump.

Ralph runs to his mother. As he reaches her side, she stumbles, rolls over and begins to snore loudly. Ralph is bewildered. This is no time to sleep. He tries to wake her, but it is no good.

Then he sees five, gangly, upright animals running towards him. He does not recognise their smell. He remembers what his mother has told him and realises they must be people.

Ralph fears the worst. These people must be poachers. Two of them carry guns. They must have swapped their land vehicle for a giant bird and come to take his mother's horns.

Ralph wants to protect his mother but he knows his small body is no match for a gun. Quickly, he scuttles off to hide behind a nearby boulder.

When they reach his mother's body, the people seem to know just what to do. They are not poachers, but game wardens. They have come to remove Rosie's horns. It is a simple and painless operation. Without her horns, the game wardens know that Rosie is unlikely to be killed by poachers.

Two of the game wardens lift Rosie's head, rest her chin on a pillow and begin to mark her horns. Another two douse Rosie's body with water to stop her overheating in the sunshine. The fifth person carefully removes the dart.

In no time at all, the game wardens have sawn off both of Rosie's horns. The last thing they do, before running back to their helicopter, is daub a sticky, black antiseptic on the bumps that were once her proud horns.

Ralph is puzzled. He does not know if the people are game wardens or poachers. Thankfully, they have not killed his mother – he can still hear her snores – and yet they have stolen her magnificent horns.

As soon as the helicopter has lifted, Ralph creeps out of his hiding place. He tries to wake Rosie but she does not stir. Tired and confused, he lies down by her side and starts to sleep.

Ralph is roused by angry snorts. His mother has woken to discover the theft of her horns. She exclaims that now it will be strange meeting other rhinos that she would normally greet with a rubbing of horns or a territorial tussle, but at least she is alive.

The game wardens have cut her horns off very neatly and she knows they will grow back again, just as Ralph's are growing now. Meanwhile, at least she does not have to fear the poachers because they are unlikely to kill her while she has no horns.

Ralph is very hungry when Rosie eventually struggles to her feet. Once again, they set off to look for the welwitschia plants. Ralph licks his lips – dinner at last.

TRUE OR FALSE?

Which of these facts are true and which ones are false? If you have read this book carefully you will know the answers.

1. The rhino's closest relative is the hippo.
2. Rhino tusks are made of ivory.
3. There are four remaining types of rhino.
4. Black rhinos are the same colour as white rhinos.

5. The Indian rhino wears an armour-plated suit.
6. The Sumatran rhino has a thin hairy coat.

7. Rhinos live on mountain slopes.
8. Rhinos like to lie in wet mud.
9. Some rhinos knock down small trees and bushes to reach the upper leaves.
10. Baby rhinos are called cubs.
11. Rhinos weigh the same as human babies at birth.
12. Indian elephants are scared of rhinos.
13. Birds visit rhinos to pick insects off their skin.
14. African rhinos sharpen their horns on rocks and trees.
15. In some countries, people believe rhinos have magical qualities.

ANSWERS: 1. False; 2. False; 3. False; 4. True; 5. False; 6. True; 7. False; 8. True; 9. True; 10. False; 11. False; 12. True; 13. True; 14. True; 15. True.

INDEX